50 Flavor Party Recipes for Home

By: Kelly Johnson

Table of Contents

- Spicy Mango Salsa with Tortilla Chips
- Honey-Sriracha Chicken Wings
- Garlic-Parmesan Stuffed Mushrooms
- Lemon-Basil Shrimp Skewers
- Smoky Chipotle Guacamole
- Sweet Chili Coconut Shrimp
- Jalapeño Poppers with Cream Cheese
- Pineapple Teriyaki Meatballs
- Zesty Lemon-Herb Roasted Potatoes
- Chili-Lime Grilled Corn on the Cob
- Maple-Bourbon Glazed Chicken Bites
- BBQ Pulled Pork Sliders
- Thai Peanut Noodle Salad
- Sweet and Spicy Bacon-Wrapped Dates
- Parmesan Crusted Zucchini Fries
- Cranberry Brie Bites
- Cumin-Lime Grilled Steak Tacos
- Mediterranean Hummus Platter
- Buffalo Cauliflower Bites
- Truffle Parmesan Popcorn
- Pomegranate Glazed Chicken Kebabs
- Caramelized Onion and Fig Flatbread
- Spicy Korean Beef Lettuce Wraps
- Sriracha-Lime Deviled Eggs
- Sweet Potato and Black Bean Quesadillas
- Creamy Jalapeño-Cilantro Dip
- Moroccan Spiced Lamb Meatballs
- Lemon-Dill Salmon Bites
- Honey Balsamic Brussels Sprouts
- Chipotle Chicken Tacos with Avocado
- Spinach and Artichoke Stuffed Bread
- Cajun Shrimp and Sausage Skewers
- Maple Mustard Glazed Carrots
- Roasted Red Pepper and Feta Dip
- Teriyaki Beef Skewers with Pineapple

- Sun-Dried Tomato and Olive Tapenade
- Cinnamon Sugar Churro Bites
- Spicy Garlic Edamame
- Prosciutto Wrapped Melon with Mint
- Bacon and Cheddar Stuffed Jalapeños
- Coconut-Curry Chicken Satay
- Sweet and Tangy BBQ Meatballs
- Sesame-Ginger Grilled Chicken Skewers
- Roasted Garlic and Herb Cream Cheese Spread
- Sweet Potato Fries with Chipotle Mayo
- Asian-Style Chicken Lettuce Wraps
- Balsamic-Glazed Caprese Skewers
- Honey Glazed Pecans with Rosemary
- Tandoori Chicken Bites
- Chimichurri Steak Crostini

Spicy Mango Salsa with Tortilla Chips

Ingredients:

- 2 ripe mangoes, peeled and diced
- 1/2 red onion, finely chopped
- 1-2 jalapeños, seeded and finely chopped (adjust to spice preference)
- 1/2 red bell pepper, diced
- 1/4 cup fresh cilantro, chopped
- Juice of 1 lime
- Salt to taste
- 1/2 teaspoon chili powder (optional for extra heat)
- Tortilla chips (store-bought or homemade)

Instructions:

1. **Prepare the Mango Salsa:**
   - In a large bowl, combine the diced mangoes, red onion, jalapeños, and red bell pepper.
   - Add the chopped cilantro and lime juice.
   - Season with salt to taste and, if desired, sprinkle in the chili powder for extra heat.
   - Gently toss all the ingredients until well mixed.
2. **Chill the Salsa:**
   - Place the salsa in the fridge for 15-20 minutes to allow the flavors to meld together.
3. **Serve:**
   - Enjoy the spicy mango salsa with crunchy tortilla chips as a flavorful snack or appetizer.

Enjoy the sweet, spicy, and tangy flavors!

Honey-Sriracha Chicken Wings

Ingredients:

- 2 lbs chicken wings
- 1/4 cup honey
- 1/4 cup Sriracha sauce
- 2 tbsp soy sauce
- 1 tbsp unsalted butter, melted
- 1 tsp garlic powder
- 1/2 tsp salt
- 1/4 tsp black pepper
- Sesame seeds and chopped green onions for garnish (optional)

Instructions:

1. **Preheat the Oven:** Preheat oven to 400°F (200°C). Line a baking sheet with foil and place a wire rack on top.
2. **Prepare the Wings:** In a large bowl, toss the chicken wings with garlic powder, salt, and pepper. Arrange the wings on the wire rack in a single layer.
3. **Bake the Wings:** Bake for 35-40 minutes, flipping halfway through, until crispy and golden.
4. **Make the Sauce:** While the wings bake, whisk together honey, Sriracha, soy sauce, and melted butter in a small saucepan. Heat over low until slightly thickened, about 2-3 minutes.
5. **Toss and Serve:** Once wings are done, toss them in the honey-Sriracha sauce. Garnish with sesame seeds and green onions if desired. Serve hot!

Garlic-Parmesan Stuffed Mushrooms

Ingredients:

- 20-24 white button mushrooms, stems removed
- 1/4 cup breadcrumbs
- 1/4 cup grated Parmesan cheese
- 2 tbsp cream cheese, softened
- 2 tbsp butter, melted
- 3 garlic cloves, minced
- 2 tbsp fresh parsley, chopped
- Salt and pepper to taste

Instructions:

1. **Preheat the Oven:** Preheat oven to 375°F (190°C). Lightly grease a baking sheet.
2. **Prepare the Mushroom Filling:** In a small skillet, melt the butter and sauté the garlic until fragrant, about 1-2 minutes. In a bowl, mix the garlic, breadcrumbs, Parmesan, cream cheese, parsley, salt, and pepper.
3. **Stuff the Mushrooms:** Spoon the mixture into the hollowed mushroom caps. Place them on the baking sheet.
4. **Bake the Mushrooms:** Bake for 15-20 minutes, until the mushrooms are tender and the filling is golden. Serve immediately as a delicious appetizer.

Lemon-Basil Shrimp Skewers

Ingredients:

- 1 lb large shrimp, peeled and deveined
- 2 tbsp olive oil
- 2 tbsp fresh lemon juice
- 1 tbsp lemon zest
- 2 garlic cloves, minced
- 1/4 cup fresh basil, chopped
- Salt and pepper to taste
- Wooden skewers (soaked in water for 30 minutes)

Instructions:

1. **Prepare the Marinade:** In a large bowl, whisk together olive oil, lemon juice, lemon zest, garlic, basil, salt, and pepper.
2. **Marinate the Shrimp:** Add the shrimp to the bowl and toss to coat. Let the shrimp marinate for 15-20 minutes.
3. **Assemble the Skewers:** Thread the shrimp onto the skewers, leaving a little space between each.
4. **Grill the Skewers:** Preheat a grill or grill pan over medium heat. Grill the shrimp skewers for 2-3 minutes per side until the shrimp are opaque and cooked through.
5. **Serve:** Serve the Lemon-Basil Shrimp Skewers hot with extra lemon wedges for squeezing. Perfect for a light and zesty meal!

Smoky Chipotle Guacamole

Ingredients:

- 3 ripe avocados
- 1 chipotle pepper in adobo, minced
- 1/2 red onion, finely chopped
- 1 garlic clove, minced
- Juice of 1 lime
- 1/4 cup fresh cilantro, chopped
- Salt and pepper to taste

Instructions:

1. **Mash the Avocados:** In a bowl, mash the avocados with a fork until slightly chunky.
2. **Mix in the Ingredients:** Add the minced chipotle, red onion, garlic, lime juice, cilantro, salt, and pepper. Mix until well combined.
3. **Serve:** Serve with tortilla chips or as a topping for tacos.

Sweet Chili Coconut Shrimp

Ingredients:

- 1 lb large shrimp, peeled and deveined
- 1/2 cup flour
- 2 eggs, beaten
- 1 cup shredded coconut
- 1/2 cup panko breadcrumbs
- 1/2 cup sweet chili sauce
- Vegetable oil for frying

Instructions:

1. **Prep the Coating:** Set up a breading station with flour, beaten eggs, and a mix of coconut and panko.
2. **Coat the Shrimp:** Dredge each shrimp in flour, dip in egg, then coat with the coconut-panko mixture.
3. **Fry the Shrimp:** Heat oil in a pan and fry shrimp until golden, about 2-3 minutes per side. Drain on paper towels.
4. **Serve:** Drizzle with sweet chili sauce and serve hot.

Jalapeño Poppers with Cream Cheese

Ingredients:

- 12 fresh jalapeños, halved and seeded
- 8 oz cream cheese, softened
- 1/2 cup shredded cheddar cheese
- 1/4 cup green onions, chopped
- 1/4 tsp garlic powder
- 12 slices bacon, halved

Instructions:

1. **Prepare the Filling:** In a bowl, mix cream cheese, cheddar, green onions, and garlic powder.
2. **Stuff the Jalapeños:** Fill each jalapeño half with the cream cheese mixture.
3. **Wrap with Bacon:** Wrap each stuffed jalapeño with a half slice of bacon.
4. **Bake:** Bake at 400°F (200°C) for 20-25 minutes, until the bacon is crispy.

Pineapple Teriyaki Meatballs

Ingredients:

- 1 lb ground beef
- 1/2 cup breadcrumbs
- 1 egg
- 1/4 cup pineapple juice
- 1/4 cup teriyaki sauce
- 1/2 tsp garlic powder
- 1/4 cup crushed pineapple

Instructions:

1. **Make the Meatballs:** Mix ground beef, breadcrumbs, egg, garlic powder, and pineapple juice. Form into meatballs.
2. **Bake the Meatballs:** Bake at 375°F (190°C) for 20 minutes.
3. **Add the Sauce:** In a pan, combine teriyaki sauce and crushed pineapple. Simmer for 5 minutes. Toss the cooked meatballs in the sauce before serving.

Zesty Lemon-Herb Roasted Potatoes

Ingredients:

- 2 lbs baby potatoes, halved
- 2 tbsp olive oil
- Juice and zest of 1 lemon
- 2 garlic cloves, minced
- 1 tbsp fresh rosemary, chopped
- Salt and pepper to taste

Instructions:

1. **Preheat the Oven:** Preheat oven to 400°F (200°C).
2. **Toss the Potatoes:** In a bowl, toss the potatoes with olive oil, lemon juice, zest, garlic, rosemary, salt, and pepper.
3. **Roast:** Spread the potatoes on a baking sheet and roast for 25-30 minutes, stirring halfway through, until golden and crispy.

Chili-Lime Grilled Corn on the Cob

Ingredients:

- 4 ears of corn, husked
- 2 tbsp butter, melted
- 1 tsp chili powder
- Juice of 1 lime
- 1/4 cup cotija cheese, crumbled
- Fresh cilantro for garnish

Instructions:

1. **Grill the Corn:** Preheat a grill and cook the corn for 10-12 minutes, turning occasionally.
2. **Make the Topping:** Mix melted butter, chili powder, and lime juice.
3. **Serve:** Brush the grilled corn with the butter mixture, sprinkle with cotija cheese, and garnish with cilantro.

Maple-Bourbon Glazed Chicken Bites

Ingredients:

- 1 lb chicken breast, cut into bite-sized pieces
- 1/4 cup maple syrup
- 2 tbsp bourbon
- 2 tbsp soy sauce
- 1 tbsp Dijon mustard
- Salt and pepper to taste

Instructions:

1. **Cook the Chicken:** In a pan, sauté chicken pieces until cooked through, about 5-7 minutes.
2. **Make the Glaze:** In a small saucepan, combine maple syrup, bourbon, soy sauce, and mustard. Simmer for 3-5 minutes until thickened.
3. **Glaze the Chicken:** Toss the cooked chicken in the maple-bourbon glaze. Serve warm.

BBQ Pulled Pork Sliders

Ingredients:

- 2 lbs pork shoulder
- 1 cup BBQ sauce
- 1/2 cup chicken broth
- 12 slider buns
- Coleslaw for topping

Instructions:

1. **Cook the Pork:** Place pork shoulder in a slow cooker with chicken broth. Cook on low for 6-8 hours until tender. Shred the pork with two forks.
2. **Mix with BBQ Sauce:** Toss the shredded pork in BBQ sauce.
3. **Assemble the Sliders:** Serve the pulled pork on slider buns with a spoonful of coleslaw on top.

Thai Peanut Noodle Salad

Ingredients:

- 8 oz rice noodles
- 1/4 cup peanut butter
- 2 tbsp soy sauce
- 2 tbsp lime juice
- 1 tbsp honey
- 1 tbsp sesame oil
- 1 garlic clove, minced
- 1/2 cup shredded carrots
- 1/2 cup red bell pepper, sliced
- 1/4 cup fresh cilantro, chopped
- 1/4 cup peanuts, chopped

Instructions:

1. **Cook the Noodles:** Prepare rice noodles according to package instructions. Drain and set aside.
2. **Make the Peanut Sauce:** In a bowl, whisk together peanut butter, soy sauce, lime juice, honey, sesame oil, and garlic.
3. **Combine the Salad:** Toss the noodles with peanut sauce, carrots, bell pepper, cilantro, and peanuts. Serve chilled or at room temperature.

Sweet and Spicy Bacon-Wrapped Dates

Ingredients:

- 12 Medjool dates, pitted
- 12 almonds
- 6 slices bacon, halved
- 1 tbsp honey
- 1/4 tsp cayenne pepper

Instructions:

1. **Stuff the Dates:** Insert an almond into each pitted date.
2. **Wrap with Bacon:** Wrap each date with half a slice of bacon and secure with a toothpick.
3. **Bake:** Place on a baking sheet and bake at 400°F (200°C) for 15-20 minutes until crispy.
4. **Glaze:** Mix honey and cayenne pepper, then drizzle over the dates before serving.

Parmesan Crusted Zucchini Fries

Ingredients:

- 2 zucchinis, cut into fries
- 1/2 cup breadcrumbs
- 1/4 cup grated Parmesan cheese
- 1 egg, beaten
- 1 tsp garlic powder
- Salt and pepper to taste

Instructions:

1. **Preheat the Oven:** Preheat oven to 425°F (220°C). Line a baking sheet with parchment paper.
2. **Coat the Zucchini:** Dip zucchini fries into beaten egg, then into a mixture of breadcrumbs, Parmesan, garlic powder, salt, and pepper.
3. **Bake:** Arrange on the baking sheet and bake for 15-20 minutes, until golden and crispy.

Cranberry Brie Bites

Ingredients:

- 1 sheet puff pastry, thawed
- 1/2 cup cranberry sauce
- 1 small wheel of brie, cubed
- Fresh thyme for garnish

Instructions:

1. **Preheat the Oven:** Preheat oven to 375°F (190°C).
2. **Prepare the Pastry:** Cut the puff pastry into 2-inch squares and press into mini muffin tins.
3. **Assemble:** Place a cube of brie and a spoonful of cranberry sauce in each pastry.
4. **Bake:** Bake for 10-12 minutes until the pastry is golden and the brie is melted. Garnish with fresh thyme.

Cumin-Lime Grilled Steak Tacos

Ingredients:

- 1 lb flank steak
- 2 tbsp olive oil
- Juice of 2 limes
- 1 tsp ground cumin
- 1 tsp chili powder
- 1 garlic clove, minced
- Salt and pepper to taste
- 8 small corn tortillas
- Toppings: cilantro, diced onions, salsa

Instructions:

1. **Marinate the Steak:** In a bowl, mix olive oil, lime juice, cumin, chili powder, garlic, salt, and pepper. Marinate the steak for 30 minutes.
2. **Grill the Steak:** Grill the steak over medium-high heat for 4-5 minutes per side. Let rest, then slice thinly.
3. **Assemble the Tacos:** Serve the steak in warm tortillas with your favorite toppings.

Mediterranean Hummus Platter

Ingredients:

- 1 cup hummus
- 1/4 cup Kalamata olives, sliced
- 1/4 cup cherry tomatoes, halved
- 1/4 cup cucumber, sliced
- 2 tbsp feta cheese, crumbled
- 2 tbsp olive oil
- 1 tsp za'atar seasoning
- Pita bread or chips for serving

Instructions:

1. **Assemble the Platter:** Spread hummus on a serving dish.
2. **Top with Ingredients:** Arrange olives, tomatoes, cucumber, and feta on top of the hummus. Drizzle with olive oil and sprinkle with za'atar.
3. **Serve:** Serve with pita bread or chips.

Buffalo Cauliflower Bites

Ingredients:

- 1 head cauliflower, cut into florets
- 1/2 cup flour
- 1/2 cup water
- 1/4 cup buffalo sauce
- 2 tbsp melted butter

Instructions:

1. **Preheat the Oven:** Preheat oven to 425°F (220°C).
2. **Coat the Cauliflower:** In a bowl, whisk flour and water into a batter. Toss cauliflower florets in the batter.
3. **Bake:** Spread the coated cauliflower on a baking sheet and bake for 20 minutes.
4. **Add the Sauce:** Mix buffalo sauce with melted butter. Toss the baked cauliflower in the sauce and bake for another 10 minutes. Serve with ranch or blue cheese dressing.

Truffle Parmesan Popcorn

Ingredients:

- 1/4 cup popcorn kernels
- 2 tbsp truffle oil
- 1/4 cup grated Parmesan cheese
- Salt to taste

Instructions:

1. **Pop the Popcorn:** Heat the popcorn kernels in a pot until fully popped.
2. **Add Truffle Oil:** Drizzle the truffle oil over the popcorn and toss to coat.
3. **Season:** Sprinkle with Parmesan cheese and salt. Toss again and serve warm.

Pomegranate Glazed Chicken Kebabs

Ingredients:

- 1 lb chicken breast, cubed
- 1/2 cup pomegranate juice
- 2 tbsp honey
- 1 tbsp olive oil
- 2 garlic cloves, minced
- 1 tsp ground cumin
- Salt and pepper to taste
- Skewers

Instructions:

1. **Make the Marinade:** In a bowl, mix pomegranate juice, honey, olive oil, garlic, cumin, salt, and pepper.
2. **Marinate the Chicken:** Add chicken cubes to the marinade and let sit for 30 minutes.
3. **Grill the Kebabs:** Thread chicken onto skewers and grill over medium heat for 10-12 minutes, turning occasionally, until cooked through. Brush with additional glaze while grilling. Serve hot.

Caramelized Onion and Fig Flatbread

Ingredients:

- 1 pre-made flatbread
- 2 large onions, thinly sliced
- 1/4 cup dried figs, sliced
- 1/2 cup goat cheese, crumbled
- 1 tbsp olive oil
- 1 tsp balsamic vinegar
- Fresh thyme for garnish

Instructions:

1. **Caramelize the Onions:** Heat olive oil in a pan and sauté onions on low heat for 20-25 minutes until golden and caramelized. Stir in balsamic vinegar and cook for another minute.
2. **Assemble the Flatbread:** Spread caramelized onions over the flatbread, top with figs and goat cheese.
3. **Bake:** Bake at 400°F (200°C) for 8-10 minutes until the edges are crisp. Garnish with fresh thyme and serve.

Spicy Korean Beef Lettuce Wraps

Ingredients:

- 1 lb ground beef
- 1/4 cup gochujang (Korean chili paste)
- 2 tbsp soy sauce
- 2 tbsp sesame oil
- 1 garlic clove, minced
- 1 tbsp ginger, minced
- 1 head of butter lettuce, leaves separated
- Sesame seeds and sliced green onions for garnish

Instructions:

1. **Cook the Beef:** In a skillet, cook ground beef with sesame oil, garlic, and ginger until browned. Drain excess fat.
2. **Add the Sauce:** Stir in gochujang and soy sauce. Cook for another 2 minutes until the sauce is well combined.
3. **Assemble the Wraps:** Serve the spicy beef in lettuce leaves and garnish with sesame seeds and green onions.

Sriracha-Lime Deviled Eggs

Ingredients:

- 6 hard-boiled eggs, halved
- 3 tbsp mayonnaise
- 1 tsp Sriracha
- 1 tsp lime juice
- Salt and pepper to taste
- Chopped cilantro for garnish

Instructions:

1. **Make the Filling:** Remove the yolks and mash them in a bowl. Add mayonnaise, Sriracha, lime juice, salt, and pepper. Mix until smooth.
2. **Fill the Eggs:** Spoon or pipe the filling into the egg whites.
3. **Garnish:** Top with chopped cilantro and serve chilled.

Sweet Potato and Black Bean Quesadillas

Ingredients:

- 1 large sweet potato, peeled and diced
- 1 can black beans, drained and rinsed
- 1/2 cup shredded cheddar cheese
- 2 tbsp olive oil
- 1/2 tsp cumin
- 1/2 tsp chili powder
- 4 large tortillas

Instructions:

1. **Cook the Sweet Potatoes:** Sauté diced sweet potato in olive oil until tender, about 8-10 minutes. Add cumin, chili powder, and black beans, and cook for another 2 minutes.
2. **Assemble the Quesadillas:** Spread sweet potato and black bean mixture on half of each tortilla, sprinkle with cheese, and fold in half.
3. **Cook the Quesadillas:** In a skillet, cook each quesadilla until crispy and golden, about 2-3 minutes per side.

Creamy Jalapeño-Cilantro Dip

Ingredients:

- 1 cup sour cream
- 1/4 cup mayonnaise
- 2 jalapeños, seeds removed
- 1/4 cup fresh cilantro
- 2 garlic cloves
- Juice of 1 lime
- Salt and pepper to taste

Instructions:

1. **Blend the Ingredients:** In a blender, combine sour cream, mayonnaise, jalapeños, cilantro, garlic, lime juice, salt, and pepper. Blend until smooth.
2. **Serve:** Chill for 30 minutes before serving with chips or veggies.

Moroccan Spiced Lamb Meatballs

Ingredients:

- 1 lb ground lamb
- 1/4 cup breadcrumbs
- 1 egg
- 2 garlic cloves, minced
- 1 tsp ground cumin
- 1 tsp ground coriander
- 1/2 tsp ground cinnamon
- Salt and pepper to taste
- Fresh mint for garnish

Instructions:

1. **Make the Meatballs:** In a bowl, combine ground lamb, breadcrumbs, egg, garlic, cumin, coriander, cinnamon, salt, and pepper. Form into small meatballs.
2. **Cook the Meatballs:** Heat a skillet over medium heat and cook meatballs for 8-10 minutes, turning occasionally, until browned and cooked through.
3. **Serve:** Garnish with fresh mint and serve with yogurt or couscous.

Lemon-Dill Salmon Bites

Ingredients:

- 1 lb salmon fillet, cut into bite-sized pieces
- 2 tbsp olive oil
- Juice of 1 lemon
- 2 tbsp fresh dill, chopped
- 1 garlic clove, minced
- Salt and pepper to taste

Instructions:

1. **Marinate the Salmon:** In a bowl, mix olive oil, lemon juice, dill, garlic, salt, and pepper. Toss salmon pieces in the marinade and let sit for 15-20 minutes.
2. **Cook the Salmon:** Preheat a grill or skillet over medium heat. Cook salmon bites for 2-3 minutes per side until cooked through.
3. **Serve:** Serve warm as an appetizer or main dish.

Honey Balsamic Brussels Sprouts

Ingredients:

- 1 lb Brussels sprouts, trimmed and halved
- 2 tbsp olive oil
- 2 tbsp honey
- 2 tbsp balsamic vinegar
- Salt and pepper to taste

Instructions:

1. **Preheat the Oven:** Preheat oven to 425°F (220°C).
2. **Prepare the Brussels Sprouts:** Toss Brussels sprouts with olive oil, honey, balsamic vinegar, salt, and pepper.
3. **Roast:** Spread on a baking sheet and roast for 20-25 minutes, stirring halfway through, until tender and caramelized.

Chipotle Chicken Tacos with Avocado

Ingredients:

- 1 lb chicken breast, diced
- 2 tbsp chipotle seasoning
- 1 tbsp olive oil
- 1 avocado, sliced
- 8 small tortillas
- Fresh cilantro for garnish

Instructions:

1. **Cook the Chicken:** In a skillet, heat olive oil over medium heat. Add chicken and chipotle seasoning. Cook until chicken is cooked through, about 5-7 minutes.
2. **Assemble the Tacos:** Serve chicken in tortillas topped with avocado slices and cilantro.

Spinach and Artichoke Stuffed Bread

Ingredients:

- 1 loaf French bread
- 1 cup cooked spinach, drained
- 1/2 cup marinated artichoke hearts, chopped
- 1/2 cup cream cheese
- 1/2 cup shredded mozzarella cheese
- 1/4 cup grated Parmesan cheese

Instructions:

1. **Prepare the Filling:** In a bowl, mix spinach, artichokes, cream cheese, mozzarella, and Parmesan.
2. **Stuff the Bread:** Slice the French bread lengthwise and spread the filling evenly over the cut sides.
3. **Bake:** Bake at 375°F (190°C) for 10-12 minutes until the cheese is melted and bubbly.

Cajun Shrimp and Sausage Skewers

Ingredients:

- 1 lb large shrimp, peeled and deveined
- 1/2 lb smoked sausage, sliced
- 2 tbsp Cajun seasoning
- 2 tbsp olive oil
- Skewers

Instructions:

1. **Prepare the Skewers:** Thread shrimp and sausage onto skewers, alternating them.
2. **Season and Cook:** Brush with olive oil and sprinkle with Cajun seasoning. Grill over medium heat for 5-7 minutes, turning occasionally, until shrimp are pink and sausage is heated through.

Maple Mustard Glazed Carrots

Ingredients:

- 1 lb baby carrots
- 2 tbsp maple syrup
- 2 tbsp Dijon mustard
- 1 tbsp olive oil
- Salt and pepper to taste

Instructions:

1. **Cook the Carrots:** In a pot of boiling water, cook carrots for 5-7 minutes until tender. Drain.
2. **Prepare the Glaze:** In a pan, heat olive oil and mix in maple syrup and Dijon mustard.
3. **Toss the Carrots:** Add carrots to the pan and toss in the glaze until well coated and heated through.

Roasted Red Pepper and Feta Dip

Ingredients:

- 1 cup roasted red peppers, chopped
- 1/2 cup feta cheese, crumbled
- 1/4 cup Greek yogurt
- 1 tbsp olive oil
- 1 garlic clove, minced
- Salt and pepper to taste

Instructions:

1. **Blend the Ingredients:** In a blender, combine roasted red peppers, feta, Greek yogurt, olive oil, garlic, salt, and pepper. Blend until smooth.
2. **Serve:** Chill before serving with pita chips or vegetables.

Teriyaki Beef Skewers with Pineapple

Ingredients:

- 1 lb beef sirloin, cut into cubes
- 1 cup teriyaki sauce
- 1 cup pineapple chunks
- 2 tbsp sesame seeds
- Skewers

Instructions:

1. **Marinate the Beef:** In a bowl, marinate beef cubes in teriyaki sauce for at least 30 minutes.
2. **Prepare the Skewers:** Thread beef and pineapple chunks onto skewers.
3. **Grill:** Grill over medium heat for 8-10 minutes, turning occasionally, until beef is cooked to your liking. Sprinkle with sesame seeds before serving.

Sun-Dried Tomato and Olive Tapenade

Ingredients:

- 1/2 cup sun-dried tomatoes, chopped
- 1/2 cup Kalamata olives, pitted and chopped
- 1/4 cup capers, drained
- 2 tbsp olive oil
- 2 garlic cloves, minced
- 1 tbsp fresh basil, chopped
- Salt and pepper to taste

Instructions:

1. **Combine Ingredients:** In a food processor, combine sun-dried tomatoes, olives, capers, olive oil, garlic, basil, salt, and pepper.
2. **Process:** Blend until smooth.
3. **Serve:** Serve with crusty bread or as a dip with vegetables.

Cinnamon Sugar Churro Bites

Ingredients:

- 1 cup all-purpose flour
- 1/2 cup water
- 1/4 cup unsalted butter
- 1/4 cup sugar
- 1/2 tsp ground cinnamon
- 2 large eggs
- Vegetable oil for frying

Instructions:

1. **Prepare the Dough:** In a saucepan, combine water, butter, and 1/4 cup sugar. Bring to a boil, then stir in flour until dough forms. Remove from heat and cool slightly.
2. **Mix in Eggs:** Beat in eggs one at a time until smooth.
3. **Fry the Bites:** Heat oil in a skillet. Drop spoonfuls of dough into the hot oil and fry until golden brown. Drain on paper towels.
4. **Coat with Cinnamon Sugar:** Combine remaining sugar and cinnamon. Toss churro bites in the mixture while still warm.

Spicy Garlic Edamame

Ingredients:

- 1 lb edamame, in pods
- 2 tbsp olive oil
- 4 garlic cloves, minced
- 1 tsp red pepper flakes
- Salt to taste

Instructions:

1. **Cook the Edamame:** Boil edamame in salted water for 5 minutes. Drain and pat dry.
2. **Sauté:** In a skillet, heat olive oil and sauté garlic and red pepper flakes until fragrant.
3. **Add Edamame:** Toss in edamame and cook for another 2-3 minutes until heated through. Season with salt.

Prosciutto Wrapped Melon with Mint

Ingredients:

- 1 cantaloupe or honeydew melon, cut into wedges
- 8 slices prosciutto
- Fresh mint leaves for garnish

Instructions:

1. **Wrap the Melon:** Wrap each melon wedge with a slice of prosciutto.
2. **Serve:** Arrange on a platter and garnish with fresh mint leaves.

Bacon and Cheddar Stuffed Jalapeños

Ingredients:

- 12 jalapeños, halved and seeded
- 1/2 cup shredded cheddar cheese
- 1/2 cup cooked bacon, crumbled
- 4 oz cream cheese, softened
- 1/4 cup chopped green onions

Instructions:

1. **Prepare the Filling:** In a bowl, mix cheddar cheese, bacon, cream cheese, and green onions.
2. **Stuff the Jalapeños:** Spoon the mixture into the jalapeño halves.
3. **Bake:** Bake at 375°F (190°C) for 15-20 minutes until the cheese is melted and bubbly.

Coconut-Curry Chicken Satay

Ingredients:

- 1 lb chicken breast, cut into strips
- 1/2 cup coconut milk
- 2 tbsp curry powder
- 1 tbsp soy sauce
- 1 tbsp honey
- Skewers

Instructions:

1. **Marinate the Chicken:** In a bowl, mix coconut milk, curry powder, soy sauce, and honey. Marinate chicken strips for at least 30 minutes.
2. **Grill the Satay:** Thread chicken onto skewers and grill over medium heat for 5-7 minutes per side until cooked through.
3. **Serve:** Serve with additional coconut milk curry sauce if desired.

Sweet and Tangy BBQ Meatballs

Ingredients:

- 1 lb ground beef
- 1/2 cup breadcrumbs
- 1/4 cup BBQ sauce
- 1 egg
- 1 tsp garlic powder
- 1/2 tsp onion powder
- 1/4 cup chopped fresh parsley

Instructions:

1. **Prepare the Meatballs:** In a bowl, mix ground beef, breadcrumbs, BBQ sauce, egg, garlic powder, onion powder, and parsley. Form into meatballs.
2. **Bake:** Place meatballs on a baking sheet and bake at 400°F (200°C) for 15-20 minutes until cooked through.
3. **Serve:** Toss with additional BBQ sauce if desired.

Sesame-Ginger Grilled Chicken Skewers

Ingredients:

- 1 lb chicken breast, cut into chunks
- 1/4 cup soy sauce
- 2 tbsp sesame oil
- 2 tbsp honey
- 1 tbsp fresh ginger, minced
- 2 garlic cloves, minced
- Sesame seeds for garnish
- Skewers

Instructions:

1. **Marinate the Chicken:** In a bowl, mix soy sauce, sesame oil, honey, ginger, and garlic. Marinate chicken chunks for at least 30 minutes.
2. **Grill the Skewers:** Thread chicken onto skewers and grill over medium heat for 5-7 minutes per side until cooked through.
3. **Serve:** Garnish with sesame seeds and serve hot.

Roasted Garlic and Herb Cream Cheese Spread

Ingredients:

- 1 head garlic
- 8 oz cream cheese, softened
- 2 tbsp fresh chives, chopped
- 2 tbsp fresh parsley, chopped
- 1 tbsp fresh thyme, chopped
- Salt and pepper to taste

Instructions:

1. **Roast the Garlic:** Preheat oven to 400°F (200°C). Cut the top off the garlic head, drizzle with olive oil, wrap in foil, and roast for 30-35 minutes until soft.
2. **Prepare the Spread:** Squeeze the roasted garlic cloves out of their skins and mix with cream cheese, chives, parsley, thyme, salt, and pepper.
3. **Serve:** Chill before serving with crackers or bread.

Sweet Potato Fries with Chipotle Mayo

Ingredients:

- 2 large sweet potatoes, peeled and cut into fries
- 2 tbsp olive oil
- 1 tsp paprika
- 1/2 tsp garlic powder
- Salt and pepper to taste
- 1/2 cup mayonnaise
- 1 tbsp chipotle hot sauce

Instructions:

1. **Prepare the Fries:** Toss sweet potato fries with olive oil, paprika, garlic powder, salt, and pepper.
2. **Bake:** Spread on a baking sheet and bake at 425°F (220°C) for 25-30 minutes, turning halfway through, until crispy.
3. **Make the Dip:** Mix mayonnaise and chipotle hot sauce. Serve alongside fries.

Asian-Style Chicken Lettuce Wraps

Ingredients:

- 1 lb ground chicken
- 2 tbsp soy sauce
- 1 tbsp hoisin sauce
- 1 tbsp sesame oil
- 2 garlic cloves, minced
- 1 tbsp fresh ginger, minced
- 1 cup water chestnuts, diced
- 1/2 cup green onions, chopped
- Butter lettuce leaves

Instructions:

1. **Cook the Chicken:** In a skillet, heat sesame oil and cook garlic and ginger until fragrant. Add ground chicken and cook until browned.
2. **Add Flavors:** Stir in soy sauce, hoisin sauce, water chestnuts, and green onions. Cook for 2-3 minutes until well combined.
3. **Assemble:** Spoon chicken mixture into lettuce leaves and serve.

Balsamic-Glazed Caprese Skewers

Ingredients:

- 1 pint cherry tomatoes
- 8 oz fresh mozzarella balls
- Fresh basil leaves
- 1/4 cup balsamic glaze
- Skewers

Instructions:

1. **Assemble Skewers:** Thread cherry tomatoes, mozzarella balls, and basil leaves onto skewers.
2. **Drizzle with Glaze:** Arrange on a platter and drizzle with balsamic glaze before serving.

Honey Glazed Pecans with Rosemary

Ingredients:

- 1 cup pecan halves
- 2 tbsp honey
- 1 tbsp olive oil
- 1 tbsp fresh rosemary, chopped
- Salt to taste

Instructions:

1. **Prepare the Pecans:** Preheat oven to 350°F (175°C). In a bowl, toss pecans with honey, olive oil, rosemary, and salt.
2. **Bake:** Spread on a baking sheet and bake for 10-12 minutes, stirring halfway through, until toasted.
3. **Serve:** Cool before serving.

Tandoori Chicken Bites

Ingredients:

- 1 lb chicken breast, cut into bite-sized pieces
- 1/2 cup plain yogurt
- 2 tbsp tandoori spice mix
- 1 tbsp lemon juice
- 1 tbsp vegetable oil

Instructions:

1. **Marinate the Chicken:** Mix yogurt, tandoori spice mix, lemon juice, and vegetable oil. Marinate chicken pieces for at least 1 hour.
2. **Grill:** Thread chicken onto skewers and grill over medium heat for 8-10 minutes, turning occasionally, until cooked through.
3. **Serve:** Serve hot with naan or rice.

Chimichurri Steak Crostini

Ingredients:

- 1 lb flank steak
- 1 tbsp olive oil
- 1/2 tsp salt
- 1/2 tsp pepper
- 1 baguette, sliced and toasted
- 1/2 cup chimichurri sauce (store-bought or homemade)

Instructions:

1. **Cook the Steak:** Rub steak with olive oil, salt, and pepper. Grill or sear in a pan over high heat for 4-5 minutes per side for medium-rare. Let rest, then slice thinly.
2. **Assemble Crostini:** Top toasted baguette slices with steak slices and a spoonful of chimichurri sauce.
3. **Serve:** Arrange on a platter and serve.